To every person who has had their life forever changed
by the unconditional love of a dog.

To Sargent the best Great Dane a girl could ever ask for.
Not a day goes by that I don't miss you and wish you were still a part of my family.
And to Jarrid, the best human a girl could ever ask for.

—Shannon

For Chris.
I will keep you in my heart and I will see you soon.

—David

Copyright © 2022 by Shannon Scharkey
Illustrated by David Gnass

All rights reserved.
No part of this book may be reproduced in any manner,
except for brief quotations in critical articles or reviews, without permission.

Big Dogs Publishing

Published by Big Dogs Publishing
United States of America

First edition 2022
Printed in China

Text layout by DTPerfect Book Design

ISBN (paperback) 979-8-9868704-1-0 | ISBN (hardcover) 979-8-9868704-0-3 | ISBN (ebook) 979-8-9868704-2-7

Follow the real Great Danes on social media
TikTok: @thegreatdanes | Instagram: @thegreatdanes6 | Facebook: @thegreatdanes6

www.thegreatdanes.org

For inquiries, contact the author at shannonscharkey@gmail.com

THE GREAT DANES
Big Dogs Living Large

Written by
Shannon Scharkey

Illustrated by
David Gnass

One day, four Great Dane puppies entered the world and everything changed.

Lola and **Tristan's** home became cramped and busy with **sixteen paws** running, playing, and learning about life.

Mack is the boss since he is the **biggest** and the **baddest**.

He loves music and takes every chance he can to **dance** and be in the **spotlight**.

Daisy is daring and loves **adventure**.

She likes to run and move **fast**.

Daisy wants to be a **racecar driver** when she grows up.

Lucy loves everyone and everything, but especially **red lollipops**. Every day is the best day for Lucy.

While Lucy is asleep and snoring loudly, she **dreams** of being a **movie star** when she grows up.

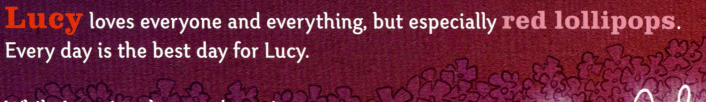

That's So Hollywood!

Griffin sometimes hides in his bed and doesn't want to come out to play.

Even though he is shy, Griffin **loves** to **sing**. He has a captive audience with his best friend Johnny the Giraffe who **loves** to hear him **sing**.

Big dogs love **big**.

They have **big** paws and **big** hearts.

But sometimes loving each other is not easy.

Like when **Mack** steals the best stick.

This Great Dane family does **everything** together . . .

from sleeping and eating **string cheese** to chasing each other through the **grass** and playing **hide-and-seek**.

But **bath time?** The puppies never enjoy that . . .

"**No way!** I am **not** taking a bath!" they scream.

Lola chases, she wrangles, and she tricks the puppies into taking their baths.

After all the **soapy suds**, **wet towels** and **fur** being blown dry with **hair dryers** is finished, and all of the Great Danes are squeaky clean and looking good, the best part comes . . .

Movie Night!

But tonight was different. With the popcorn popped and ready, the Great Danes settled in for a fun night on the couch.

"What's happened? Why is this couch suddenly so small?"

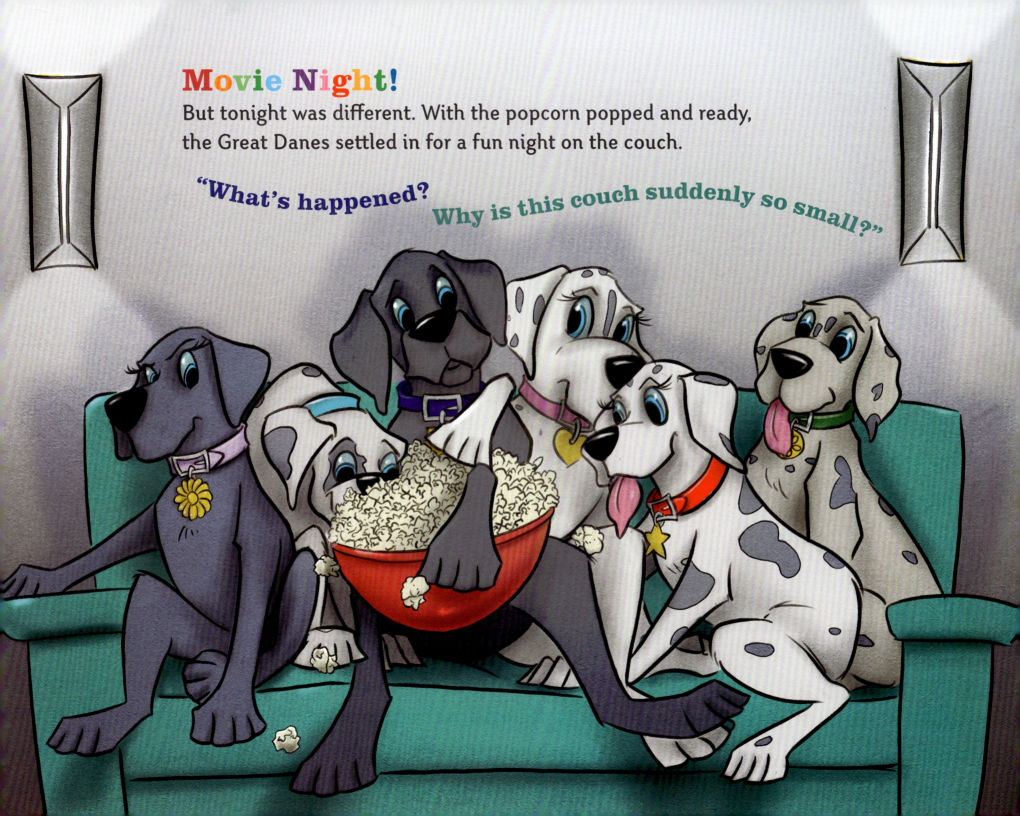

"**Mom!**

We do not fit in the **doorway** anymore!"

Tristan wants a car with lots of room.

Lola wants the car to have all the best safety features to protect the family.

Daisy wants a fast car.

Mack wants a big car.

Griffin wants a car with a sunroof so he can feel the wind in his hair.

Lucy just wants a red car to match her lollipops.

And now, in the new car they all love, the Great Danes are ready for their next big adventure.

"I think we are going to need a bigger house," Lola whispers.

The End, but really just the beginning.

Who Is Your Favorite Great Dane?

Mack
Nickname: Dancy Pants
Personality: Confident, Silly, Entertainer
Favorite Activity: Dancing
Favorite Color: Blue
Favorite Food: Popcorn
Dreams of Becoming a Dance Contest Winner

Griffin
Nickname: Sloppy Kisses
Personality: Goofy, Bashful, Affectionate
Favorite Activity: Singing
Favorite Color: Green
Favorite Food: Macaroni and Cheese
Dreams of Becoming a Rock Star

Tristan
Nickname: The Sarge
Personality: Fun Loving, Responsible, Loyal
Favorite Activity: Playing Sports
Favorite Color: Yellow
Favorite Food: French Toast
Dreams of Becoming a Professional Basketball Player

Daisy

Nickname: Crazy Daisy
Personality: Daring, Funny, Adventurous
Favorite Activity: Running in the Rain
Favorite Color: Purple
Favorite Food: Pizza
Dreams of Becoming a Race Car Driver

Lucy

Nickname: Lucy Lollipop
Personality: Sweet, Kind, Joyful
Favorite Activity: Playing in the Snow
Favorite Color: Red
Favorite Food: Candy
Dreams of Becoming a Movie Star

Lola

Nickname: Diva Dane
Personality: Devoted, Artistic, Protective
Favorite Activity: Sunbathing at the Beach
Favorite Color: Pink
Favorite Food: Cheesy Baked Potatoes
Dreams of Becoming an Award Winning Artist